Poems and Prose 1949–1977

Poems and Prose
1949-1977

by HAROLD PINTER

Eyre Methuen Ltd. London

To Antonia

Contents

POEMS

PROSE

Poems

New Year in the Midlands

Now here again she blows, landlady of lumping
Fellows between the boards,
Singing 'O Celestial Light', while
Like a T-square on the
Flood swings her wooden leg.
This is the shine, the powder and blood, and here am I,
Straddled, exile always in one Whitbread Ale town,
Or such.
Where we went to the yellow pub, cramped in an alley bin,
A shoot from the market,
And found the thin Luke of a queer, whose pale
Deliberate eyes, raincoat, Victorian,
Sap the answer in the palm.
All the crush, camp, burble and beer
Of this New Year's Night; the psalm derided;
The black little crab women with the long
Eyes, lisp and claw in a can of chockfull stuff.
I am rucked in the heat of treading; the well-rolled
Sailor boys soon rocked to sleep, whose ferret fig
So calms the coin of a day's fever.
Now in this quaver of a roisty bar, the wansome lady
I blust and stir,
Who pouts the bristle of a sprouting fag—
Sprinkled and diced in these Midland lights
Are Freda the whimping glassy bawd, and your spluttered guide,

I

Blessed with ambrosial bitter weed. —Watch
How luminous hands
Unpin the town's genitals—
Young men and old
With the beetle glance,
The crawing brass whores, the clamping
Red shirted boy, ragefull, thudding his cage.

1950

The Midget

I saw the midget in the ringing airs,
That night upon the crest.
The bowed trees, the silent beast,
Under the wind.

And saw the voyagers stand stiff,
Deathsure, stiff and coffined
In that still place,
Hands clasped, tall hats on.

1950

Christmas

Choose the baby's cocktail,
To drink in an eartrumpet.
Deprivation angers; at least
Rejoice in his captivity.

Give Maurice lemons.
He's broken the pottery,
Arses round the attic,
Gorging biscuits and olives.

This is a happy family.
Come, sing of the harbour,
Nights guzzling bouillabaisse.
We'll syringe to the next flat,
Make another party.

1950

Chandeliers and Shadows

'I'le goe hunt the badger by owle-light: 'tis a deed of darknesse.'
The Duchess of Malfi

The eyes of a queen germinate
In this brothel, in this room,
The kings are fled, the potentates
Shuffle kingdoms with the sweet fingers.
Mountains, kingdoms, valets erudite,
Muffling flaunts of deliverate ecstasy
Slips, shoves, the deluded whore,
The hectoring mice, the crabs of lemon,
Scrawled thick tails across the stateroom.
Masks gape in the floodlit emperies,
Where wax violins, donkey splendour falls,
The brocaded gown of servants and moths,
The horsefly, the palsied stomacher,
Worlds dying, suns in delirium,
Catch the sleek counsellor,
Hold the crystal elixir of muffs.

Enwrapped in this crust, this crumpled mosaic,
Camphor and rosefall stifle the years,
Yet I, lunatic from lunatic spheres,
Shall run crazy with lepers,
And bring God down the chimney,

A tardy locust,
To plunder and verminate man's pastures, entirely.
Sudden I stay blinded with Orion's menace,
The sky cuts the ice-shell
With the strip and fall of a darting star,
The split, the splintered palace.
Let tham all burn together
In a trite December,
A necromantic cauldron of crosses,
And on Twelfth Night the long betrayed monster
Shall gobble their gilded gondolas.

1950

Hampstead Heath

I, lying on grass, lie
in the thunderclapping moment,
eradicate voice
in the green limit.

Stone in the fruitwomb,
world under grass,
alone under alone.

Suggested lines my body
consume, in the day's graph.
Note the brown ant
in his blade jungle.

I am my pupil's blank, rule
out of magnitude the ant,
decrease the seed's activity
this blunt minute.

Below the transparent fly
insect equation quite strides
the slim glass of word,
instructs the void.

Exterior tricks: the click
of bush; the oblong trade
of noise; the posture of these
high boughs.

1951

I shall tear off my Terrible Cap

I in my strait jacket swung in the sun,
In a hostile pause in a no man's time.
The spring his green anchor had flung.
Around me only the walking brains,
And the plack of their onelegged dreams
As I hung.

I tell them this—
Only the deaf can hear and the blind understand
The miles I gabble.
Through these my dances of dunce and devil,
It's only the dumb can speak through the rubble.
Time shall drop his spit in my cup,
With this vicious cut he shall close my trap
And gob me up in a drunkard's lap.
All spirits shall haunt me and all devils drink me;
O despite their dark drugs and the digs that they rib me,
I'll tear off my terrible cap.

1951

A Glass at Midnight

Time of the mongrel at my foot
Scraping for a coin that's born
In the carpet in a grave of hair.

Miles of the poles in the room's corners.
The eskimostars in an octagon. Worlds
Within this box.

I hold the cipher of the voided world,
Four fingers holding the sea in a glass,
Incumbent an arm on the ashtray table.

Time in the tughoot night stops
A religion that grows on the window.
I let the glass drop. A bridge falls.
Flatten the midnight on the fingered tightrope.
All the dumb days draw on.

1951

Book of Mirrors

My book is crammed with the dead
Youths of years.

Fabulous in image I walked the Mayworlds,
Equal in favour the concubant winds,
Set by my triangle the sectant sounds,
Till crowed lips I kissed,
Supped with a blood of snapping birds,
In a doom and ring of belladonna to sleep.

Spruced, I welcomed their boneating smiles,
Till I grew bound and easy with ills,
Strewing for decorance a hundred grails.
And anger-rich with gallows and banks,
The world raped on her back,
From the shanks of my widowing kids
I played Adam's uncle's joke.

In the house of my heart spawned
The invited doves.
May springroot slum their hurt limbs,
That they chirp the early ladies
And prop the mad brideworld up.
May they breathe sweet; the shapes
That ounced my glad weight

With ripe and century fingers,
That locked the skeleton years
With a gained grief.

1951

The Islands of Aran seen from the Moher Cliffs

The three whales of Aran
Humped in the sun's teeth,
Make tough bargain with the cuff
And statement of the sea.

I stand on Moher, the cliffs
Like coalvaults, see Aran
In mourning thumped to losses
By its season's neighbour.

Aran like three black whales
Humped on the water,
With a whale's barricade
Stares out the waves.

Aran with its bleak gates locked,
Its back to the traders,
Aran the widower,
Aran with no legs.

Distended in distance
From the stone of Connemara's head,
Aran without gain, pebbled
In the fussing Atlantic.

1951

The Drama in April

So March has become a museum,
And the April curtains move.
I travel the vacant gallery
To the last seat.
In the spring décor
The actors pitch tents,
In a beak of light
Begin their play.

Their cries in the powdered dark
Assemble in mourning over
Ambassadors from the wings.
And objects and props in the rain
Are the ash of the house
And the grave unnumbered stones
In the green.

I move to the interval,
Done with this repertory.

1952

Jig

Seeing my portholed women
Fall on the murdered deck,
I rage in my iron cabin.

Faster my starboard women,
Spun by the metal breeze,
Dance to a cut-throat temper.

Seeing my men in armour
Brand the galley bark,
I skip to drydock.

Women and men together,
All in a seaquick temper,
Tick the cabin clock.

1952

The Anaesthetist's Pin

The anaesthetist's pin
Binds up the bawl of pain.
The amputator's saw
Breaks the condition down.

In the division of blood
That stems the fractured bow,
The wrist-attacking hound
Snipes out the stair below.

At that incision sound
The lout is at the throat
And the dislocated word
Becomes articulate.

1952

Camera Snaps

The politician tricks the mouse,
Whose bites are rancid
In that aloed wound.
The sun's in the cabinet.

The sun's in the cabinet.
That drudge undoes the skeleton,
And chops the scientific dug.
Light across the picture.

Dark across the picture.
The basement midget, rabid
As the stoat, periscopes
The tickshop of the moon.

The churchman at his game
Unrolls his fishing-line,
Jabs an even pool.
Dark across the cabinet.

1952

You in the Night

You in the night should hear
The thunder and the walking air.
You on that shore shall bear
Where mastering weathers are.

All that honoured hope
Shall fail upon the slate,
And break the winter down
That clamours at your feet.

Though the enamouring altars burn,
And the deliberate sun
Make the eagle bark,
You'll tread the tightrope.

c. 1952

The Second Visit

My childhood vampire wallows in those days,
Where panting sea threatened and surf was flint,
And consummate doves flanked the eyes.

Now an actor in this nocturnal sink,
The strip of lip is toothed away,
And flats and curtains canter down.

So grows in stream of planetary tides
The sun abundant in hanging sands.

And aquiline weapons barb and fanged
Conceive amid their holy jaws
An echoed Siberia in the mind,
Where the comet fist had crushed,
And sent back trees to a gulped barrenness.

Denebola and Alphard like countertenors
Sing, and their malicious minstrels of song
Silence the tongue's gush,
And the quick opus of thighs.

My childhood vampire unpacks a new stay,
But I defy and send him off to war,
On the credit of Leo and his gods,
Against the fallingdown parents
Devoured by children, and the toy Czars.

*c.*1952

Stranger

That you did barter
And consort with her.
That you did ash
The fire at her departure.
That you did enter
Where I was unechoed.
That you did venture
Where I was a stranger.
That you did cajole
When the pendulum hung.
That you interposed
In her curious dream.
That you did instruct
From your alphabet home.
That you did confusion
Her eyelid to stone.
That you so did render
The echo unheard
That you might divide
When the echo was gone.
That you did condition
Her widowhood on.
That you were the stranger
That strangered the calm.
That you did engender

The thunder to storm.
That yours was the practise—

No case.

1953

A Walk by Waiting

A walk by listening.
A walk by waiting.

Wait under the listening
Winter, walk by the glass.

Rest by the glass of waiting.
Walk by the season of voices.

Number the winter of flowers.
Walk by the season of voices.

Wait by the voiceless glass.

1953

Poem

I walked one morning with my only wife,
Out of sandhills to the summer fair,
To buy a window and a white shawl,
Over the boulders and the sunlit hill.
But a stranger told us the fair had passed,
And I turned back with my only wife.

And I turned back and I led her home.
She followed me closely out of the summer,
Over the boulders and the moonlit hill,
Into sandhills in the early evening,
And went to our home without a window,
And the long year moved from the east.

My only wife sat by a candle.
The winter keened at the door.
A widow brought us a long black shawl.
I placed it on my true wife's shoulders.
The widow went from us into sandhills,
Away from our home without a window.

The year turned to an early sunrise.
I walked one morning with my only wife,
Out of sandhills to the summer fair,
To sell a candle and a black shawl.
We parted ways on the sunlit hill,
She silent, I to the farther west.

1953

The Task

The last time Kullus, seen,
Within a distant call,
Arrived at the house of bells,
The leaf obeyed the bud,
I closed the open night
And tailormade the room.

The last time Kullus, known,
Obeyed a distant call,
Within the house of night,
The leaf alarmed the bud,
I closed the open bell
And tailormade the room.

The last time Kullus saw
The sun upon the bough,
And in a distant call,
The bud about to break,
I set about my task
And tailormade the room.

The last time Kullus saw
The flower begin to fail,
He made a distant call,
The bud became a bell,
I disobeyed that cry
And pacified the room.

1954

The Error of Alarm

A woman speaks:
A pulse in the dark
I could not arrest.
The error of alarm
I could not dismiss.
A witness to that bargain
I could not summon.

If his substance tautens
I am the loss of his blood.
If my thighs approve him
I am the sum of his dread.

If my eyes cajole him
That is the bargain made.
If my mouth allays him
I am his proper bride.

If my hands forestall him
He is deaf to my care.
If I own to enjoy him
The bargain's bare.

The fault of alarm
He does not share.
I die the dear ritual
And he is my bier.

1956

Daylight

I have thrown a handful of petals on your breasts.
Scarred by this daylight you lie petalstruck.
So your skin imitates the flush, your head
Turning all ways, bearing a havoc of flowers over you.

Now I bring you from dark into daytime,
Laying petal on petal.

1956

Afternoon

Summer twisted from their grasp
After the first fever.
Daily from the stews
They brought the men.
And placed a wooden peg
Into the wound they had made,
And left the surgery of skin
To barbers and students.

Some burrowed for their loss
In the ironmonger's bin,
Impatient to reclaim,
Before the journey start,
Their articles of faith.

Some nosed about in the dirt,
Deaf to the smell of heat
And the men at the rubber pit,
Who scattered the parts of a goat
For their excitement and doubt.

One blind man they gave
A demented dog to sniff,
A bitch that had eaten the loot.
The dog, bare to his thought,
Became his mastiff at night,
His guardian the thief of his blood.

1957

A View of the Party

The thought that Goldberg was
A man she might have known
Never crossed Meg's words
That morning in the room.

The thought that Goldberg was
A man another knew
Never crossed her eyes
When, glad, she welcomed him.

The thought that Goldberg was
A man to dread and know
Jarred Stanley in the blood
When, still, he heard his name.

While Petey knew, not then,
But later, when the light
Full up upon their scene,
He looked into the room.

And by morning Petey saw
The light begin to dim
(That daylight full of sun)
Though nothing could be done.

ii

Nat Goldberg, who arrived
With a smile on every face,
Accompanied by McCann,
Set a change upon the place.

The thought that Goldberg was
Sat in the centre of the room,
A man of weight and time,
To supervise the game.

The thought that was McCann
Walked in upon this feast,
A man of skin and bone,
With a green stain on his chest.

Allied in their theme,
They imposed upon the room
A dislocation and doom,
Though Meg saw nothing done.

The party they began,
To hail the birthday in,
Was generous and affable,
Though Stanley sat alone.

The toasts were said and sung,
All spoke of other years,
Lulu, on Goldberg's breast,
Looked up into his eyes.

And Stanley sat—alone,
A man he might have known,
Triumphant on his hearth,
Which never was his own.

For Stanley had no home.
Only where Goldberg was,
And his bloodhound McCann,
Did Stanley remember his name.

They played at blind man's buff,
Blindfold the game was run,
McCann tracked Stanley down,
The darkness down and gone

Found the game lost and won,
Meg, all memory gone,
Lulu's lovenight spent,
Petey impotent;

A man they never knew
In the centre of the room,
And Stanley's final eyes
Broken by McCann.

1958

The Table

I dine the longest
All this time

My feet I hear
Fall on the fat

On cheese and eggs
On weekend bones

The sound of light
Has left my nose.

Tattooed with all
I could not see

I whisper in
My deafest ear

My name erased
Was sometime here

Or total bluff
Preserved its care.

To this enchained
With this in love

I move on fours
Without a word

And stuffed with tributes
Hog the scraps

Breathless,
Under this enormous table.

1963

Poem

Always where you are
In what I do
Turning you hold your arms

My touch lies where you turn
Your look is in my eyes

Turning to clasp your arms
You hold my touch in you

Touching to clasp in you
The one shape of our look
I hold your face to me

Always where you are
My touch to love you looks into your eyes.

1964

All of That

All of that I made
And, making, lied.
And all of that I hid
Pretended dead.

But all of that I hid
Was always said,
But, hidden, spied
On others' good.

And all of that I led
By nose to bed
And, bedding, said
Of what I did

To all of that that cried
Behind my head
And, crying, died
And is not dead.

1970

Poem

they kissed I turned they stared
with bright eyes turning to me blind
I saw that here where we were joined
the light that fell upon us burned
so bright the darkness that we shared
while they with blind eyes turning to me turned
and I their blind kiss formed

1971

Later

Later. I look out at the moon.
I lived here once.
I remember the song.

Later. No sound here.
Moon on linoleum.
A child frowning.

Later. A voice singing.
I open the back door.
I lived here once.

Later. I open the back door
Light gone. Dead trees.
Dead linoleum. Later.

Later. Blackness moving very fast.
Blackness fatly.
I live here now.

1974

Poem

and all the others
wary now
attentive to flowers

and all the others
unsmiling
recalling others

smiling in gardens
attentive to flowers
wary now

who recall others
wary now
tendering flowers

who recall faces of others
recalling others
unwary in gardens

who tender their gardens
recalling others
wary with flowers

1974

Paris

The curtain white in folds,
She walks two steps and turns,
The curtain still, the light
Staggers in her eyes.

The lamps are golden.
Afternoon leans, silently.
She dances in my life.
The white day burns.

1975

I know the place

I know the place.
It is true.
Everything we do
Corrects the space
Between death and me
And you.

1975

Message

Jill. Fred phoned. He can't make tonight.
He said he'd call again, as soon as poss.
I said (on your behalf) OK, no sweat.
He said to tell you he was fine,
Only the crap, he said, you know, it sticks,
The crap you have to fight.
You're sometimes nothing but a walking shithouse.

I was well acquainted with the pong myself,
I told him, and I counselled calm.
Don't let the fuckers get you down,
Take the lid off the kettle a couple of minutes,
Go on the town, burn someone to death,
Find another tart, give her some hammer,
Live while you're young, until it palls,
Kick the first blind man you meet in the balls.

Anyway he'll call again.

I'll be back in time for tea.

Your loving mother.

1977

The Doing So

It is the test they set that will not go,
The failing of the doing so,
Ungainly legacy that they bestow.

I know the tricks and yet I cannot show
Why you and I in all our afterglow
Just fail the test of doing so.
It is the legacy that they bestow,
And they remorselessly will have it so.

It is the test of those who cannot row
Upon a burning sea where charred winds blow
The ghastly empires of the dead and tow
Them to their ghastly deaths to show
Them dead and ghastly, smiling, slow.
It is the test they set that will not go.

And all our dead and all their dead friends know
We have no gift for lying low,
No gift at all for doing so.
The test they set you will not go.
It is the legacy that they bestow,
The failing of the doing so.

1977

44

Denmark Hill

Well, at least you're there,
And when I come into the room,
You'll stand, your hands linked,
And smile,
Or, if asleep,
Wake.

September 1977

Prose

Kullus

I

I let him in by the back door.
There was a brisk moon.
 —Come in.
He stepped inside, slapping his hands, into the room.
 —Go on Kullus. Go to the fire.
He stooped to the grate and stretched his fingers.
 —You do not welcome warmth,
said Kullus.
 —I?
 —There is no meeting. There is separation.
 —I have no bias.
 —You have a bias,
replied Kullus.

You are biased towards cold. But you shut out cold and do not acknowledge warmth. This can on no account be named a fire. It is merely another aspect of light and shade in this room. It is not committed to its ordained activity. It does not move from itself, for want of an attention and discernment necessary to its growth. You live an avoidance of both elements.

 —Sit down Kullus. Take a seat.
 —I am not alone.
 —Oh?
 —I am to call, should you permit it.
I sat down on my stool.
 —Call.
At the door, Kullus called. Soon a girl was in the room, shawled. I nodded.

51

She nodded. She bent at the grate, remained, rose, looked at Kullus.

    —Here, *said Kullus.*

She went to him. They climbed into my bed. I placed a coat over the lamp, and watched the ceiling hustle to the floor. Then the room moved to the flame in the grate. I shifted my stool and sat by the flame in the grate.

II

Kullus took a room. The window was closed, if it was warm, and open, if it was cold. The curtains were open, if it was night, and closed, if it was day. Why closed? Why open?

    —I have my night,

said Kullus.

      I have my day.

    —Do you live far from here?

asked the girl.

Kullus then opened the curtains. For the curtains were open, if it was cold, and closed if it was warm.

I stretched my fingers to the grate.

Why open? Why closed?

    —I know cold,

said Kullus.

      I know its neighbour. Sit down. You are alone.

And so I sat down on the stool, which he placed for me.

    —You have no fire here,

I said.

Kullus moved away.

I looked at the girl. She spoke to me alone.

    —Why don't you move in here?

she asked.

—Is it possible?

—Can you move in here?

said the girl.

—But how could I?

—I will close the curtains,

said the girl.

—But now it is night.

—I cannot close them alone.

—It is Kullus's night.

—Which is your room?

said the girl.

III

The curtains were closed. I crouched far from the fire.

—What has happened to Kullus?

I asked.

He has changed.

In her room I crouched far from the fire.

—What has happened to Kullus?

She remained close to the grate.

—You did not move in here,

she said.

—No.

—Which is your room?

she said.

—I am no longer in my room.

The cold turned to the corner.

—Why are you shawled?

asked the girl, and opened the curtains.

53

The brisk moon and the cold turned to the corner.
    —What has happened to you?
said the girl.
    You have changed.
The ceiling hustled to the floor.
    —You have not shifted the coat from the lamp,
I said.

1949

The Black and White

I always catch the all-night bus, six days out of the week. I walk to Marble Arch and get the two-nine-four, that takes me to Fleet Street. I never speak to the men on the all-night buses. Then I go into the Black and White at Fleet Street and sometimes my friend comes. I have a cup of tea. She is taller than me but thinner. Sometimes she comes and we sit at the top table. I always keep her place but you can't always keep it. I never speak to them when they take it. Some remarks I never listen to. A man slips me the morning paper sometimes, the first one. He told me what he was once. I never go down to the place near the Embankment. I did go down there once. You can see what goes on from the window by the top table if you look. Mostly it's vans. They're always rushing. Mostly they're the same van-drivers, sometimes they're different. My brother was the same. He used to be in on it. But I can do better without the night, when it's dark, it's always light in the Black and White, sometimes it's blue, I can't see much. But I can do better without the cold when it's cold. It's always warm in the Black and White, sometimes it's draughty, I don't kip. Five o'clock they close down to give it a scrub round. I always wear my grey skirt and my red scarf, you never see me without lipstick. Sometimes my friend comes, she always brings over two teas. If there's someone taken her place she tells him. She's older than me but thinner. If it's cold I might have soup. You get a good bowl. They give you the slice of bread. They won't do that with tea but they do it with soup. So I might have soup, if it's cold. Now and again you can see the all-night buses going down. They all run down there. I've never been the other way, not the way some of them go. I've been down to Liverpool Street. That's where some of them end up. She's greyer than me. The lights get you down a bit. Once a man stood up and made a speech. A copper came in. They got him out. Then the copper came over to us. We soon told him off, my friend did. I never seen him since, either of them. They don't get many coppers. I'm a bit old for that, my

57

friend told him. Are you, he said. Too old for you, she said. He went.
I don't mind, there's not too much noise, there's always a bit of noise.
Young people in cabs come in once. She didn't like the coffee. I've never
had the coffee. I had coffee up at Euston, a time or two, going back. I
like the vegetable soup better than the tomato. I was having a bowl then
and this man was leaning from across the table, dead asleep, but sitting
on his elbows, scratching his head. He was pulling the hairs out of his
head into my soup, dead asleep. I pulled my bowl away. But at five
o'clock they close down to give it a scrub round. They don't let you
stay. My friend never stays, if she's there. You can't buy a cup of tea.
I've asked but they won't let you sit, not even with your feet up. Still,
you can get about four hours out of it. They only shut hour and a half.
You could go down to that one near the Embankment, but I've only
been down there once. I've always got my red scarf. I'm never without
lipstick. I give them a look. They never pick me up. They took my
friend away in the wagon once. They didn't keep her. She said they took
a fancy to her. I've never gone in for that. You keep yourself clean.
Still, she won't stand for any of it in the Black and White. But they
don't try much. I see them look. Mostly nobody looks. I don't know
many, some I've seen about. One woman in a big black hat and big
black boots comes in. I never make out what she has. He slips her the
morning paper. It's not long. You can go along, then come back. When
it's light I go. My friend won't wait. She goes. I don't mind. One got
me sick. Came in a fur coat once. They give you injections, she said, it's
all Whitehall, they got it all worked out, she said, they can tap your
breath, they inject you in the ears. My friend came later. She was a bit
nervy. I got her quiet. They'd take her in. When it's light I walk up to
the Aldwych. They're selling the papers. I've read it. One morning I
went a bit over Waterloo Bridge. I saw the last two-nine-six. It must
have been the last. It didn't look like an all-night bus, in daylight.

1954–55

The Examination

When we began, I allowed him intervals. He expressed no desire for these, nor any objection. And so I took it upon myself to adjudge their allotment and duration. They were not consistent, but took alteration with what I must call the progress of our talks. With a chalk I kept I marked the proposed times upon the blackboard, before the beginning of a session, for him to examine, and to offer any criticism if he felt so moved. But he made no objection, nor, during our talks, expressed any desire for a break in the proceedings. However, as I suspected they might benefit both of us, I allowed him intervals.

The intervals themselves, when they occurred, at whatever juncture, at whatever crucial point, preceded by whatever deadlock, were passed, naturally, in silence. It was not uncommon for them to be both preceded and followed by an equal silence, but this is not to say that on such occasions their purpose was offended. Frequently his disposition would be such that little could be achieved by insistence, or by persuasion. When Kullus was disposed to silence I invariably acquiesced, and prided myself on those occasions with tactical acumen. But I did not regard these silences as intervals, for they were not, and neither, I think, did Kullus so regard them. For if Kullus fell silent, he did not cease to participate in our examination. Never, at any time, had I reason to doubt his active participation, through word and through silence, between interval and interval, and I recognized what I took to be his devotion as actual and unequivocal, besides, as it seemed to me, obligatory. And so the nature of our silence within the frame of our examination, and the nature of our silence outside the frame of our examination, were entirely opposed.

Upon my announcement of an interval Kullus would change, or act in such a manner as would suggest change. His behaviour, on these occasions, was not consistent, nor, I am convinced, was it initiated by motives of resentment or enmity, although I suspect Kullus was aware of my watchfulness. Not that I made any pretence to be otherwise. I was obliged to remark, and, if possible, to verify, any ostensible change in his manner, whether it was outside the frame of our examination or not. And it is upon this point that I could be accused of error. For gradually it appeared that these intervals proceeded according to his terms. And where both allotment and duration had rested with me, and had become my imposition, they now proceeded according to his dictates, and became his imposition.

For he journeyed from silence to silence, and I had no course but to follow. Kullus's silence, where he was entitled to silence, was compounded of numerous characteristics, the which I duly noted. But I could not always follow his courses, and where I could not follow, I was no longer his dominant.

Kullus's predilection for windows was not assumed. At every interval he retired to the window, and began from its vantage, as from a source. On approaching initially, when the break was stated, he paid no attention to the aspect beyond, either in day-time or in night-time. And only in his automatic course to the window, and his lack of interest in the aspect beyond, did he prove consistent.

Neither was Kullus's predilection for windows a deviation from former times. I had myself suffered under his preoccupation upon previous occasions, when the order of his room had been maintained by particular arrangement of window and curtain, according to day and to night, and seldom to my taste or my comfort. But now he maintained no such order and did not determine their opening or closing. For we were no longer in Kullus's room.

And the window was always open, and the curtains were always open.

Not that Kullus displayed any interest in this constant arrangement, in the intervals, when he might note it. But as I suspect he was aware of my watchfulness, so I suspect he was aware of my arrangement. Dependent on the intensity of his silence I could suspect and conclude, but where his silence was too deep for echo, I could neither suspect nor conclude. And so gradually, where this occurred, I began to take the only course open to me, and terminated the intervals arbitrarily, cutting short the proposed duration, when I could no longer follow him, and was no longer his dominant.

But this was not until later.

When the door opened. When Kullus, unattended, entered, and the interim ended. I turned from all light in the window, to pay him due regard and welcome. Whereupon without reserve or hesitation, he moved from the door as from shelter, and stood in the light from the window. So I watched the entrance become vacant, which had been his shelter. And observed the man I had welcomed, he having crossed my border.

Equally, now, I observed the selected properties, each in its place; the blackboard, the window, the stool. And the door had closed and was absent, and of no moment. Imminent upon opening and welcoming it had possessed moment. Now only one area was to witness activity and to suffer procedure, and that only was necessary and valid. For the door was closed and so closed.

Whereupon I offered Kullus the stool, the which I placed for him. He showed, at this early juncture, no disregard for my directions; if he did not so much obey, he extended his voluntary co-operation. This was sufficient for my requirements. That I detected in him a desire for a summation of our efforts spoke well for the progress of our examination. It was my aim to avoid the appearance of subjection; a common policy, I understand, in like examinations. Yet I was naturally dominant, by virtue of my owning the room; he having entered through the door I now closed. To be confronted with the especial properties of my abode, bearing the seal and arrangement of their tenant, allowed only for recognition on the part of my visitor, and through recognition to acknowledgement, and through acknowledgement to appreciation, and through

63

appreciation to subservience. At least, I trusted that such a development would take place, and initially believed it to have done so. It must be said, however, that his manner, from time to time, seemed to border upon indifference, yet I was not deluded by this, or offended. I viewed it as a utility he was compelled, and entitled, to fall back on, and equally as a tribute to my own incisiveness and patience. And if then I viewed it as a tactical measure, it caused me little concern. For it seemed, at this time, that the advantage was mine. Had not Kallus been obliged to attend this examination? And was not his attendance an admission of that obligation? And was not his admission an acknowledgement of my position? And my position therefore a position of dominance? I calculated this to be so, and no early event caused me to re-assess this calculation. Indeed, so confident was I in the outcome of our talks, that I decided to allow him intervals.

To institute these periods seemed to me both charitable and politic. For I hoped he might benefit from a period of no demand, so be better equipped for the periods of increased demand which would follow. And, for a time, I had no reason to doubt the wisdom of this arrangement. Also, the context of the room in which Kullus moved during the intervals was familiar and sympathetic to me, and not so to him. For Kullus had known it, and now knew it no longer, and took his place in it as a stranger, and when each break was stated, was compelled to pursue a particular convention and habit in his course, so as not to become hopelessly estranged within its boundaries. But gradually it became apparent that only in his automatic course to the window, and his lack of interest in the aspect beyond, did he prove consistent.

Prior to his arrival, I had omitted to establish one property in the room, which I knew to be familiar to him, and so liable to bring him ease. And never once did he remark the absence of a flame in the grate. I concluded he did not recognize this absence. To balance this, I emphasized the presence of the stool, indeed, placed it for him, but as he never once remarked this presence, I concluded his concern did not embrace it. Not that it was at any time simple to determine by what particular his concern might be engaged. However, in the intervals, when I was able to observe him with possibly a finer detachment, I hoped to determine this.

Until his inconsistency began to cause me alarm, and his silence to confound me.

I can only assume Kullus was aware, on these occasions, of the scrutiny of which he was the object, and was persuaded to resist it, and to act against it. He did so by deepening the intensity of his silence, and by taking courses I could by no means follow, so that I remained isolated, and outside his silence, and thus of negligible influence. And so I took the only course open to me, and terminated the intervals arbitrarily, cutting short the proposed duration, when I could no longer follow him, and was no longer his dominant.

For where the intervals had been my imposition, they had now become his imposition.

Kullus made no objection to this adjustment, though without doubt he noted my anxiety. For I suffered anxiety with good cause, out of concern for the progress of our talks, which now seemed to me to be affected. I was no longer certain whether Kullus participated in our examination, nor certain whether he still understood that as being the object of our meeting. Equally, the nature of our silences, which formerly were distinct in their opposition; that is, a silence within the frame of our examination, and a silence outside the frame of our examination; seemed to me no longer opposed, indeed were indistinguishable, and were one silence, dictated by Kullus.

And so the time came when Kullus initiated intervals at his own inclination, and pursued his courses at will, and I was able to remark some consistency in his behaviour. For now I followed him in his courses without difficulty, and there was no especial duration for interval or examination, but one duration, in which I participated. My devotion was actual and unequivocal. I extended my voluntary co-operation, and made no objection to procedure. For I desired a summation of our efforts. And when Kullus remarked the absence of a flame in the grate, I was bound to acknowledge this. And when he remarked the presence of the stool, I was equally bound. And when he removed the blackboard, I offered no criticism. And when he closed the curtains I did not object.

For we were now in Kullus's room.

1955

Tea Party

I wrote this short story in 1963, and in 1964 was commissioned by the B.B.C. to write a play for the European Broadcasting Union. I decided to treat the same subject in play form. In my view, the story is the more successful.

My eyes are worse.

My physician is an inch under six feet. There is a grey strip in his hair, one, no more. He has a brown stain on his left cheek. His lampshades are dark blue drums. Each has a golden rim. They are identical. There is a deep black burn in his Indian carpet. His staff is bespectacled, to a woman. Through the blinds I hear the birds of his garden. Sometimes his wife appears, in white.

He is clearly sceptical on the subject of my eyes. According to him my eyes are normal, perhaps even better than normal. He finds no evidence that my sight is growing worse.

My eyes are worse. It is not that I do not see. I do see.

My job goes well. My family and I remain close friends. My two sons are my closest friends. My wife is closer. I am close friends with all my family, including my mother and my father. Often we sit and listen to Bach. When I go to Scotland I take them with me. My wife's brother came once, and was useful on the trip.

I have my hobbies, one of which is using a hammer and nails, or a screwdriver and screws, or various saws, on wood, constructing things or making things useful, finding a use for an object which appears to have no value. But it is not so easy to do this when you see double, or when you are blinded by the object, or when you do not see at all, or when you are blinded by the object.

My wife is happy. I use my imagination in bed. We love with the light on. I watch her closely, she watches me. In the morning her eyes shine. I can see them shining through her spectacles.

All winter the skies were bright. Rain fell at night. In the morning the skies were bright. My backhand flip was my strongest weapon. Taking position to face my wife's brother, across the dear table, my bat lightly clasped, my wrist flexing, I waited to loosen my flip to his forehand, watch him (*shocked*) dart and be beaten, flounder and sulk. My forehand was not so powerful, so swift. Predictably, he attacked my forehand. There was a ringing sound in the room, a rubber sound in the walls. Predictably, he attacked my forehand. But once far to the right on my forehand, and my weight genuinely disposed, I could employ my backhand flip, unanswerable, watch him flounder, skid and be beaten. They were close games. But it is not now so easy when you see the pingpong ball double, or do not see it at all or when, hurtling towards you at speed, the ball blinds you.

I am pleased with my secretary. She knows the business well and loves it. She is trustworthy. She makes calls to Newcastle and Birmingham on my behalf and is never fobbed off. She is respected on the telephone. Her voice is persuasive. My partner and I agree that she is of inestimable value to us. My partner and my wife often discuss her when the three of us meet for coffee or drinks. Neither of them, when discussing Wendy, can speak highly enough of her.

On bright days, of which there are many, I pull the blinds in my office in order to dictate. Often I touch her swelling body. She reads back, flips the page. She makes a telephone call to Birmingham. Even were I, while she speaks (holding the receiver lightly, her other hand poised for notes) to touch her swelling body, her call would still be followed to its

70

conclusion. It is she who bandages my eyes, while I touch her swelling body.

I do not remember being like my sons in any way when I was a boy. Their reserve is remarkable. They seem stirred by no passion. They sit silent. An odd mutter passes between them. I can't hear you, what are you saying, speak up, I say. My wife says the same. I can't hear you, what are you saying, speak up. They are of an age. They work well at school, it appears. But at pingpong both are duds. As a boy I was wide awake, of passionate interests, voluble, responsive, and my eyesight was excellent. They resemble me in no way. Their eyes are glazed and evasive behind their spectacles.

My brother in law was best man at our wedding. None of my friends were at that time in the country. My closest friend, who was the natural choice, was called away suddenly on business. To his great regret, he was therefore forced to opt out. He had prepared a superb speech in honour of the groom, to be delivered at the reception. My brother in law could not of course himself deliver it, since it referred to the long-standing friendship which existed between Atkins and myself, and my brother in law knew little of me. He was therefore confronted with a difficult problem. He solved it by making his sister his central point of reference. I still have the present he gave me, a carved pencil sharpener, from Bali.

The day I first interviewed Wendy she wore a tight tweed skirt. Her left thigh never ceased to caress her right, and vice versa. All this took place under her skirt. She seemed to me the perfect secretary. She listened to my counsel wide-eyed and attentive, her hands calmly clasped, trim, bulgy, plump, rosy, swelling. She was clearly the possessor of an active and inquiring intelligence. Three times she cleaned her spectacles with a silken kerchief.

After the wedding my brother in law asked my dear wife to remove her glasses. He peered deep into her eyes. You have married a good man, he said. He will make you happy. As he was doing nothing at the time I invited him to join me in the business. Before long he became my partner, so keen was his industry, so sharp his business acumen.

Wendy's commonsense, her clarity, her discretion, are of inestimable value to our firm.

With my eye at the keyhole I hear goosing, the squeak of them. The slit is black, only the sliding gussle on my drum, the hiss and flap of their bliss. The room sits on my head, my skull creased on the brass and loathsome handle I dare not twist, for fear of seeing black screech and scrape of my secretary writhing blind in my partner's paunch and jungle.

My wife reached down to me. Do you love me, she asked. I do love you, I spat into her eyeball. I shall prove it yet, I shall prove it yet, what proof yet, what proof remaining, what proof not yet given. All proof. (For my part, I decided on a more cunning, more allusive strategem). Do you love me, was my counter.

The pingpong table streaked with slime. My hands pant to gain the ball. My sons watch. They cheer me on. They are loud in their loyalty. I am moved. I fall back on strokes, on gambits, long since gone, flip, cut, chop, shtip, bluff to my uttermost. I play the ball by nose. The twins hail my efforts gustily. But my brother in law is no chump. He slams again, he slams again, deep to my forehand. I skid, flounder, stare sightless into the crack of his bat.

Where are my hammers, my screws, my saws?

How are you? asked my partner. Bandage on straight? Knots tight?

The door slammed. Where was I? In the office or at home? Had someone come in as my partner went out? Had he gone out? Was it silence I heard, this scuffle, creak, squeal, scrape, gurgle and muff? Tea was being poured. Heavy thighs (Wendy's? my wife's? both? apart? together?) trembled in stilletos. I sipped the liquid. It was welcome. My physician greeted me warmly. In a minute, old chap, we'll take off those bandages. Have a rock cake. I declined. The birds are at the bird bath, called his white wife. They all rushed to look. My sons sent something flying. *Someone?* Surely not. I had never heard my sons in such good form. They chattered, chuckled, discussed their work eagerly with their uncle. My parents were silent. The room seemed very small, smaller than I had remembered it. I knew where everything was, every particular. But its smell had altered. Perhaps because the room was overcrowded. My wife broke gasping out of a fit of laughter, as she was wont to do in the early days of our marriage. Why was she laughing? Had someone told her a joke? Who? Her sons? Unlikely. My sons were discussing their work with my physician and his wife. Be with you in a minute, old chap, my physician called to me. Meanwhile my partner had the two women half stripped on a convenient rostrum. Whose body swelled most? I had forgotten. I picked up a pingpong ball. It was hard. I wondered how far he had stripped the women. The top halves or the bottom halves? Or perhaps he was now raising his spectacles to view my wife's swelling buttocks, the swelling breasts of my secretary. How could I verify this? By movement, by touch. But that was out of the question. And could such a sight possibly take place under the eyes of my own children? Would they continue to chat and chuckle, as they still did, with my physician? Hardly. However, it was good to have the bandage on straight and the knots tight.

1963

73

Mac

Anew McMaster *was born in County Monaghan on Christmas Eve 1894 and was 16 when he made his first stage appearance as 'The Aristocrat' in* The Scarlet Pimpernel *with Fred Terry at the New Theatre, London. He died in Dublin on August 25th, 1962, a few days after appearing in the 'dream scene' from* The Bells *at an Equity concert. His acting career had spanned half a century and his death was the end of an era. He was the last of the great actor-managers, unconnected with films and television.*

I've been the toast of twelve continents and eight hemispheres! Mac said from his hotel bed. I'll see none of my admirers before noon. Marjorie, where are my teeth? His teeth were brought to him. None before noon, he said, and looked out of the window. If the clergy call say I am studying King Lear and am not to be disturbed. How long have you been studying King Lear, Mac? Since I was a boy. I can play the part. It's the lines I can't learn. That's the problem. The part I can do. I think. What do you think? Do you think I can do it? I wonder if I'm wise to want to do it, or unwise? But I will do it. I'll do it next season.

Don't forget I was acclaimed for my performance in Paddy The Next Best Thing. Never forget that. Should I take Othello to the Embassy, Swiss Cottage? Did you know Godfrey Tearle left out the fit? He didn't do the fit. I'm older than Godfrey Tearle. But I do the fit. Don't I? At least I don't leave it out. What's your advice? Should I take Othello to the Embassy, Swiss Cottage? Look out the window at this town. What a stinking diseased abandoned Godforgotten bog. What am I playing tonight, Marjorie? The Taming of the Shrew? But you see one thing the Irish peasantry really appreciate is style, grace and wit. You have a lovely company, someone said to me the other day, a lovely company, all the boys is like girls. Joe, are the posters up? Will we pack out? I was just driving into the town and I had to brake at a dung heap. A cow looked in through the window. No autographs today, I said. Let's have a drop of whiskey, for Jesus' sake.

Pat Magee phoned me from Ireland to tell me Mac was dead. I decided to go to the funeral. At London Airport the plane was very late leaving. I hadn't been in Ireland for ten years. The taxi raced through Dublin. We passed the Sinn Fein Hall, where we used to rehearse five plays in two weeks. But I knew I was too late for the funeral. The cemetery was

77

empty. I saw no one I knew. I didn't know Mrs. Mac's address. I knew no one any more in Dublin. I couldn't find Mac's grave.

I toured Ireland with Mac for about two years in the early 1950's. He advertised in 'The Stage' for actors for a Shakespearian tour of the country. I sent him a photograph and went to see him in a flat near Willesden Junction. At the time Willesden Junction seemed to me as likely a place as any to meet a manager from whom you might get work. But after I knew Mac our first meeting place became more difficult to accept or understand. I still wonder what he was doing interviewing actors at Willesden Junction. But I never asked him. He offered me six pounds a week, said I could get digs for twenty-five shillings at the most, told me how cheap cigarettes were and that I could play Horatio, Bassanio and Cassio. It was my first job proper on the stage.

Those two? It must be like two skeletons copulating on a bed of corrugated iron. (The actor and actress Mac was talking about were very thin). He undercuts me, he said, he keeps coming in under me. I'm the one who should come under. I'm playing Hamlet. But how can I play Hamlet if he keeps coming under me all the time? The more under I go the more under he goes. Nobody in the audience can hear a word. The bugger wants to play Hamlet himself, that's what it is. But he bloodywell won't while I'm alive. When I die I hope I die quickly. I couldn't face months of bedpans. Sheer hell. Days and months of bedpans. Do you think we'll go to heaven? I mean me. Do you think I'll go to heaven? You never saw me play the Cardinal. My cloak was superb, the length of the stage, crimson. I had six boys from the village to carry it. They used to kiss my ring every night before we made our entrance. When I made my tour of Australia and the southern hemisphere we were the guests of honour at a city banquet. The Mayor stood up. He said: We are honoured today to welcome to our city one of the most famous actors in the world, an actor who has given tremendous pleasure to people all over the world, to worldwide acclaim. It is my great privilege to introduce to you—Andrew MacPherson!

Joe Nolan, the business manager, came in one day and said: Mac, all the cinemas in Limerick are on strike. What shall I do? Book Limerick! Mac said. At once! We'll open on Monday. There was no theatre in the town. We opened on the Monday in a two thousand seater cinema, with Othello. There was no stage and no wingspace. It was St. Patrick's night. The curtain was supposed to rise at nine o'clock. But the house wasn't full until eleven thirty, so the play didn't begin until then. It was well past two in the morning before the curtain came down. Everyone of the two thousand people in the audience was drunk. Apart from that, they weren't accustomed to Shakespeare. For the first half of the play, up to 'I am your own for ever', we could not hear ourselves speak, could not hear our cues. The cast was alarmed. We expected the audience on stage at any moment. We kept our hands on our swords. I was playing Iago at the time. I came offstage with Mac at the interval and gasped. Don't worry, Mac said, don't worry. After the interval he began to move. When he walked onto the stage for the 'Naked in bed, Iago, and not mean harm' scene (his great body hunched, his voice low with grit), they silenced. He tore into the fit. He made the play his and the place his. By the time he had reached 'It is the very error of the moon; She comes more near the earth than she was wont, And makes men mad.', (the word 'mad' suddenly cauterized, ugly, shocking) the audience was quite still. And sober. I congratulated Mac. Not bad, he said, was it? Not bad. Godfrey Tearle never did the fit, you know.

Mac gave about half a dozen magnificent performances of Othello while I was with him. Even when, on the other occasions, he conserved his energies in the role, he always gave the patrons their moneysworth. At his best his was the finest Othello I have seen. His age was always a mystery, but I would think he was in his sixties at the time. Sometimes, late at night, after the show, he looked very old. But on stage in Othello he stood, well over six foot, naked to the waist, his gestures complete, final, nothing jagged, his movement of the utmost fluidity and yet of the utmost precision: stood there, dead in the centre of the role, and the great sweeping symphonic playing would begin, the rare tension and release within him, the arrest, the swoop, the savagery, the majesty and repose. His voice was unique: in my experience of an unequalled range. A bass of extraordinary echo, resonance and gut, and remarkable sweep up into tenor, when the note would hit the back of the gallery and come straight back, a brilliant, stunning sound. I remember his delivery of this line: 'Methinks (bass) it should be now a huge (bass) eclipse (tenor) of sun and moon (baritone) and that th'affrighted glove (bass) Should yawn (very deep, the abyss) at alteration.' We all watched him from the wings.

He was capable, of course, of many indifferent and offhand performances. On these occasions an edgy depression and fatigue hung over him. He would gabble his way through the part, his movement fussed, his voice acting outside him, the man himself detached from its acrobatics. At such times his eyes would fix upon the other actors, appraising them coldly, emanating a grim dissatisfaction with himself and his company. Afterwards, over a drink, he would confide: I was bad tonight, wasn't I, really awful, but the damn cast was even worse. What a lot.

He was never a good Hamlet and for some reason or other rarely bothered to play Macbeth. He was obsessed with the lighting in Macbeth and more often than not spent half his time on stage glaring at the spot bar. Yet there was plenty of Macbeth in him. I believe his dislike of the play was so intense he couldn't bring himself to play it.

It was consistent with him that after many months of coasting through Shylock he suddenly lashed fullfired into the role at an obscure matinee in a onehorse village; a frightening performance. Afterwards he said to me: What did I do? Did you notice? I did something different. What did you think of it? What was it I did? He never did it again. Not quite like that. Who saw it?

In the trial scene in The Merchant Of Venice one night I said to him (as Bassanio) instead of 'For thy three thousand ducats here is six', quite involuntarily, 'For thy three thousand *buckets* here is six'. He replied quietly and with emphasis: 'If every *bucket* in six thousand *buckets* were in six parts, and every part a *bucket* I would not draw them—I would have my bond'. I could not continue. The other members of the court scene and I turned upstage. Some walked into the wings. But Mac stood, remorseless, grave, like an eagle, waiting for my reply.

Sometimes after a matinee of Macbeth and an evening of Othello we all stayed on stage, he'd get someone to put on a record of Faust, disappear behind a curtain, reappear in a long golden wig, without his teeth, mime Marguerite weaving, mime Faust and Mephistopheles, deliver at full tilt the aria from Verdi's Othello 'Era La Notte e Cassio Dormia', while the caretaker swept the dust up, and then in a bar talk for hours of Sarah and Mrs. Pat Campbell, with relish, malice and devotion. I think he would still be talking about them now, if he wasn't dead, because they did something he knew about.

In order to present Oedipus the company had to recruit extras from the town or village we were in. One night in Dundalk Mac was building up to his blind climax when one of the extras had an epileptic fit on stage and collapsed. He was dragged to the wings where various women attended to him. The sounds of their ministrations seeped onto the stage. Mac stopped, turned to the wings and shouted: 'For God's sake, can't you see I'm trying to act!'

His concentration was always complete in Oedipus. He was at his best in the part. He acted with acute 'underness' and tenacity. And he never used his vocal powers to better or truer effect. He acted along the spine of the role and never deviated from it. As in his two other great roles, Othello and Lear, he understood and expressed totally the final tender clarity which is under the storm, the blindness, the anguish. For me his acting at these times embodied the idea of Yeats' line: 'They know that Hamlet and Lear are gay, Gaiety transfiguring all that dread'. Mac entered into this tragic gaiety naturally and inevitably.

He did Lear eventually. First performance somewhere in County Clare, Ennis, I think. Knew most of the lines. *Was* the old man, tetchy, appalled, feverish. Wanted the storm louder. All of us banged the thundersheets. No, they can still hear me. Hit it, hit it. He got above the noise. I played Edgar in Lear only a few times with him before I left the company. At the centre of his performance was a terrible loss, desolation, silence. He didn't think about doing it, he just got there. He did it and got there.

His wife, Marjorie, was his structure and support. She organized the tours, supervised all business arrangements, sat in the box office, kept the cast in order, ran the wardrobe, sewed, looked after Mac, was his dresser, gave him his whiskey. She was tough, critical, cultivated, devoted. Her spirit and belief constituted the backbone of the company. There would have been no company without her.

Ireland wasn't golden always, but it was golden sometimes and in 1950 it was, all in all, a golden age for me and for others.

The people came down to see him. Mac travelled by car, and sometimes some of us did too. But other times we went on the lorry with the flats and props, and going into Bandon or Cloughjordan would find the town empty, asleep, men sitting upright in dark bars, cow-pads, mud, smell of peat, wood, old clothes. We'd find digs; wash basin and jug, tea, black pudding, and off to the hall, set up a stage on trestle tables, a few rostra, a few drapes, costumes out of the hampers, set up shop, and at night play, not always but mostly, to a packed house (where had they come from?); people who listened, and who waited to see him, having seen him before, and been brought up on him.

Mac wasn't any kind of dreamer. He was remote from the Celtic Twilight. He kept a close eye on the box office receipts. He was sharp about money, was as depressed as anyone else when business was bad. Where there was any kind of company disagreement he proved elusive. He distanced himself easily from unwelcome problems. Mrs. Mac dealt with those. Mac was never 'a darling actor of the old school'. He was a working man. He respected his occupation and never stopped learning about it, from himself and from others.

For those who cared for him and admired him there must remain one great regret; that for reasons I do not understand, he last played in England, at Stratford, in 1933. The loser was the English theatre.

Mac wasn't 'childlike' in temperament, as some have said. He was evasive, proud, affectionate, mischievous, shrewd, merry, cynical, sad and could be callous. But he was never sour or selfpitying. His life was the stage. Life with a big L came a bad second. He had no patience with what he considered a world of petty sufferings, however important they might seem to the bearer. He was completely unsentimental. Gossip delighted him, and particularly sexual gossip. He moved with great flexibility and amusement through Catholic Ireland, greatly attracted by the ritual of the Church. He loved to speak of the mummy of the Blessed Oliver Plunkett in Drogheda 'with a lovely amber spot on its face'. He mixed freely with priests and nuns, went to Mass, sometimes, but despised the religious atrophy, rigidity and complacency with which he was confronted. He mixed with the priests partly because he enjoyed their company, partly because his livelihood depended upon them. He was a realist. But he possessed a true liberality of spirit. He was humble. He was a devout anti-puritan. He was a very great piss-taker. He was a great actor and we who worked with him were the luckiest people in the world and loved him.

1966

Hutton and the Past

HARDSTAFF and Simpson at Lords. Notts versus Middlesex. 1946 or 1947. After lunch, Keeton and Harris had opened for Notts. Keeton swift, exact, interested; Harris Harris. Harris stonewalled five balls in the over for no particular reason and hit the sixth for six, for no particular reason. Keeton and Harris gave Notts a fair start. Stott, at number three, smacked the ball hard, was out in the early afternoon. Simpson joined Hardstaff. Both very upright in their stance. They surveyed the field, surveyed themselves, began to bat.

The sun was strong, but calm. They settled into the afternoon, no hurry, all in order. Hardstaff clipped to mid-wicket. They crossed. Simpson guided the ball between midoff and the bowler. They crossed. Their cross was a trot, sometimes a walk, they didn't need to run. They placed their shots with precision, they knew where they were going. Bareheaded. Hardstaff golden. Simpson dark. Hardstaff offdrove, silently, Simpson to deep square leg. Simpson cut. Hardstaff cut, finer. Simpson finer. The slips, Robertson, Bennett, attentive. Hardstaff hooked, immaculate, no sound. They crossed, and back. Deep square leg in the heat after it. Jim Sims on at the pavilion end with leg breaks. Hardstaff wristed him into the covers. Simpson to fine leg. Two. Sims twisting. Hardstaff wristed him into the covers, through the covers, fielder wheeling, for four. Quite unhurried. Seventy in 90 minutes. No explosions. Batsmanship. Hardstaff caught at slip, off Sims.

Worrell and Weekes at Kingston on Thames. 1950. The Festival. Headley had flicked, showed what had been and what remained of himself, from the Thirties. Worrell joined Weekes with an hour to play. Gladwin and Jackson bowling. Very tight, very crisp, just short of a length, jolting, difficult. Worrell and Weekes scored 90 before close of play. No sixes, nothing off the ground. Weekes smashed, red-eyed, past cover, smashed to long leg, at war, met Gladwin head on, split midwicket in two, steel. Worrell wanted to straight drive to reach his 50. Four men at the sight screen to stop him. He straight drove, pierced them, reached his 50. Gladwin bowled a stinging ball, only just short, on middle and leg. Only sensible course was to stop it. Worrell jumped up, both feet off, slashed it from his stomach, square cut for four, boundary first bounce.

MCC versus Australians. Lords 1948. Monday. On the Saturday the Australians had plastered the MCC bowling, Barnes 100, Bradman just short. On Monday morning Miller hit Laker for five sixes into the Tavern. The Australians passed 500 and declared. The weather darkened. MCC 30 minutes batting before lunch. The Australians came into the field chucking the ball hard at each other, broad, tall, sure. Hutton and Robertson took guard against Lindwall and Miller. Robertson caught Tallon off Miller. Lindwall and Miller very fast. The sky black. Edrich caught Tallon off Miller. Last ball before lunch. MCC 20 for 2.

After lunch the Australians, arrogant, jocular, muscular, larking down the pavilion steps. They waited, hurling the ball about, eight feet tall. Two shapes behind the pavilion glass. Frozen before emerging a split second. Hutton and Compton. We knew them to be the two greatest English batsmen. Down the steps together, out to the middle. They played. The Australians quieter, wary, tight. Bradman studied them. They stayed together for an hour before Compton was out, and M. P. Donnelly, and Hutton, and the Australians walked home.

First Test at Trent Bridge. The first seven in the English batting order: Hutton, Washbrook, Edrich, Compton, Hardstaff, Barnett, Yardley. They'll never get them out, I said. At lunch on the first day, England 78 for 8.

Hutton.

England versus New Zealand 1949. Hutton opened quietly, within himself, setting his day in order. At the first hour England 40 for none. Hutton looking set for a score. Burtt, slow left hand, took the ball at the

Nursery end, tossed it up. To his first ball Hutton played a superb square drive to Wallace at deep point. Wallace stopped it. The crowd leaned in. Burtt again. Hutton flowed into another superb square drive to Wallace's right hand. Wallace stopped it. Back to the bowler. Burtt again, up. Hutton, very hard a most brilliant square drive to Wallace's left hand. Wallace stopped it. Back to the bowler. The crowd. Burtt in, bowled. Hutton halfway up the pitch immediately, driving straight. Missed it. Clean bowled. On his heel back to the pavilion.

Hutton was never dull. His bat was part of his nervous system. His play was sculptured. His forward defensive stroke was a complete statement. The handle of his bat seemed electric. Always, for me, a sense of his vulnerability, of a very uncommon sensibility. He never just went through the motions, nothing was glibly arrived at. He was never, for me, as some have defined him, simply a 'master technician'. He attended to the particular but rarely lost sight of the context in which it took place. But one day in Sydney he hit 37 in 24 minutes and was out last ball before lunch when his bat slipped in hitting a further four, when England had nothing to play for but a hopeless draw, and he's never explained why he did *that*. I wasn't there to see it and probably regret that as much as anything. But I wasn't surprised to hear about it, because every stroke he made surprised me.

I heard about Hutton's 37 on the radio. 7 a.m. Listened to every morning of the 1946/47 series. Alan McGilvray talking. Always England six wickets down and Yardley 35 not out. But it was in an Irish kitchen in County Galway that, alone, I heard Edrich and Compton in 1953 clinch the Ashes for England.

Those were the days of Bedser and Wright, Evans, Washbrook and Gimblett, M. P. Donnelly, Smailes and Bowes, A. B. Sellars, Voce and Charley Barnett, A. W. Wellard, S. M. Brown and Jim Sims, Mankad, Mustaq Ali, Athol Rowan, even H. T. Bartlett, even Hammond and certainly Bradman.

One morning at drama school I pretended illness and pale and shaky walked into Gower St. Once round the corner I jumped on a bus and ran into Lords at the Nursery end to see through the terraces Washbrook late cutting for four, the ball skidding towards me. That beautiful evening Compton made 70.

But it was 1950 when G. H. G. Doggart missed Walcott at slip off Edrich and Walcott went on to score 165, Gomez with him. Christiani was a very good fielder. Ramadhin and Valentine had a good season. Hutton scored 202 not out against them and against Goddard bowling breakbacks on a bad wicket at the Oval.

It was 1949 when Bailey caught Wallace blindingly at silly mid on. And when was it I watched Donnelly score 180 for the Gents versus Players? He went down the afternoon with his lightning pulls.

Constantine hitting a six over fine leg into the pavilion. Talk of a schoolboy called May.

1969

The Coast

I saw him again today. He looked older.

We walked, as we always used to do, along the promenade, up to the pier, along the pier, back down the pier, and back. He was more or less more or less the same, but looked older. I asked him if I had changed. He said no, as far as he could see. I said no, probably I had not. He said he could see no sign of it, if anything I looked younger. I charged him with jesting. He said no he was not. He pointed out that he had used the phrase *if anything*. *If anything*, he said, and turned his eyes, still bright, on me, *if anything* you look younger, *if anything*. If anything you look older, I said. There's no if anything about that, he retorted, none whatsoever.

We took the path we always took, wetter than ever along the cliff. Seems wetter than ever down here, he said, uproar in the Channel? How can you put up with such louzy weather? After all these years? Doesn't it oppress you? Not at all, I replied, most congenial, suits me. Do you still have nightmares? he asked. I smiled, into the wind. I haven't had a dream since 1956, I said. Bloody shocking racket you used to make, he said, drowning or something, God what an aggravation. He spat into the fret. One hour in this bloody wet end of the world is enough for me, don't know how you've survived, but nevertheless I'm glad to see you blossoming. Blossoming, I said, no, not quite that, surely, you're jesting.

But he had stopped talking. He was looking down at the sea, the sea he had known so well, the roar of our youth.

He bought me tea at the railway station. I then walked with him to his train. Glad to see you've found your feet, he said, glad to see you're blossoming. I clasped his hand and thanked him for making the journey.

1975

Problem

The phone rings. I ignore it. It persists. I'm not a fool. The stratagem I employ comes easily to me. I lift the extension. I say nothing. Silence too, at his end. He replaces his receiver. Remarkably harsh dialling tone.

After seeing to a few odd jobs I decide to make a telephone call. I lift the phone. Dead silence. Unprecedented. The telephone system in my area normally sans pareil. At the report of the slightest fault telephone technicians arrive post haste, on the dot, to correct. But in this case problem palpable. I can't phone to declare the fault, the fault is so vast, so pervasive, it so consumes, is so final, as to obstruct, without a chink of hope, aid.

Silent phone. Dead night.
The extension? Phone off hook? The extension phone off hook? I investigate. Extension secure, with a certain indolence, on hook. I am nonplussed. Not only that. I take one of my seats and sit nonplussed.

Nonplussed. No tone. Dead night.

It rings.

———————

I leave the library, go into a phone box and dial my flat. Number engaged.

———————

Someone is trying to do me in.

1976

Lola

After he had gone, I pondered on all he was evidently keeping from me. The information I had received from him was insufficient for me to do more than subject it to the broadest and most superficial analysis. The information I had received from him, meagre, banal, threadbare, misleading or, where precise, outlandish, did me in fact precious little damn bloody good. He was on a train, he said, leaving the Gare de Lyon; dozens of lines crossed; an exquisite arrangement of train upon train, crossing, deflecting, genuflecting, quite the most courteous choreography ever encountered by the witness, who then remarked the lurching silver train, undoubtedly bound for the Côte d'Azur, cheek to cheek with his own, and in the azure window (sunset, or dawn, scattered upon the pane) the darkeyed, darkhaired girl he had known, and loved, when a boy, long gone, long last seen, dancing so lightly in his young arms, amid flowering plants. It was love at second sight, confirmed, tattooed between them on golden windows (a moment when dawn and sunset glided together in summer must) her eyes her hair so lost in shocking seconds graze of light on departing Paris gone. But that can not be all. He has left me to ponder on all he has kept from me.

Saw Smith again. What rubbish. Why do I go there? Up his old stairs, the long wait for the door to open, the door opens, always the hesitation, oh hello, door kept ajar, oh hello, oh it's you, what a surprise, thought it was Lola, come in, we go in, we stand, thought it might be Lola, you can never tell when she might take it into her head to embark on another sally, sit down, sit, sit, tell me, willy nilly, all that is momentous in your life.

I tell him this: I am very happy in my house in the country and my life as a countryman. I enjoy long walks by the side of the river. It is autumn. The life of the countryside delights me, the life of birds, of ducks. I watch boys fishing. They often fish with their fathers, at their side tins of sandwiches cut by their mothers. There is no end to boats. They disappear upstream in a long wake. So easeful their progress, wide their wake. There is no scar on my landscape. I gain no pleasure whatsoever from my journeys to London, apart from seeing my oldest friend, you. I remain so closely interested in you. I think of you late at night, in my study, over my brandy. I imagine you sitting amid your candles and lilies, keeping your solitary wake. No candle I know holds a candle to your candles.

I think that I might write of you, make of you the central figure of a modest novella; modest since I doubt I could ever fully capture the heart of your character, never precisely clench you within my noose, so to speak. I see you only in the shuddering of candles, an old man, one who had never known boyhood, or other distinctions of light. My respect for you rests in the fact that you do not waver, that your patience does not waver, since, your life rapidly failing, you sit in your room paying unwavering attention to the Lola of your wavering candles. My contempt for you follows from this. My contempt for you rests in the fact that you wait only for tightskirted Lola to enter, wait only for the exquisite collision of you with her bouncing flamboyant bellbottomed bottom, the collision that will be the end of you.

He responds: Tell me more about the train incident.

What train incident?

The incident which contained a darkeyed darkhaired girl, in a train leaving Paris, in a window, passing. A dawning sunset. You both had loved, years before. She looked at you, through grazing light. You saw. She had not forgotten you. When you had last seen her she cried, you touched her wrist, she buried her head, you withdrew your hand. All this took place miles away, long before you embarked on your trip to this room.

Can I for much longer tolerate the insults to which he subjects me?

1977